BEDROOMS · CHIMNEYS AND LAVATORIES!

The Development of Hertfordshire Houses from Shelters to Homes

BY ARTHUR JONES

HERTFORDSHIRE PUBLICATIONS
1984

THIS HANDBOOK is intended to increase the interest and pleasure of all who are attracted by the history and diversity of the buildings around them. It relates particularly to the situation in Hertfordshire, and although it does have a wider relevance materials and styles differ elsewhere.

The title — BEDROOMS, CHIMNEYS AND LAVATORIES — draws attention to three developments which above all others have helped to transform the primitive shelters of our ancestors into comfortable homes:

—1—

The provision of separate rooms for sleeping and other purposes, first at one end of an open hall and later on an upper floor.

—2—

The introduction of a duct or chimney to provide an efficient exit for the smoke from the hearth. This made life more tolerable generally. It also made it possible for the upper floor to extend across the entire house.

—3—

The development of plumbing, to carry water into the house and to enable waste products to flow out of it.

It should be remembered that most of the comforts we now enjoy were already known to the Romans. Their larger houses were divided into several rooms, some of which could be centrally heated by the circulation of hot air beneath the floors and through ducts in the walls. A bath suite was usually provided, but bathing involved the use of oil and steam, since soap was unknown.

These Roman skills and standards of comfort were not carried forward into the Dark Ages which followed.

Now read on!

THROUGHOUT the Iron Age, including the period of Roman occupation, the majority of the native British population can be assumed to have lived in simple huts, open from floor to rafters, which provided shelter but little comfort. In lowland areas, walls would have been framed in light timbers and filled in with turf or woven branches, possibly coated with clay. Smoke from open fires found its own way out through openings in the thatched roof.

The main characteristics of these huts — low walls, small apertures, and enveloping roofs — remained a feature of simple cottages throughout medieval times. Examples can still be found, particularly in eastern parts of the county, built as late as the 17th century.

Meanwhile the Anglo-Saxons had introduced a type of hut with a floor excavated a foot or so below ground level, and a thatched roof supported on a ridge-pole. Its purpose is not fully understood, and the style did not remain a lasting influence on house design.

The Saxons' more enduring contribution was the development of the timber-built hall, of which no examples have been found in Hertfordshire. It was the forerunner of the aisled barns and hall houses of which many examples remain from the post-Norman period.

This reconstruction of a pre-Roman Iron Age hut, at the Chiltern Open Air Museum near Rickmansworth, is based on archaeological evidence from Dunstable. Huts of similar type were still in use after the Roman period.

WESTMILL, BUTTON SNAP

FURNEUX PELHAM.
PHEASANT HALL COTTAGES

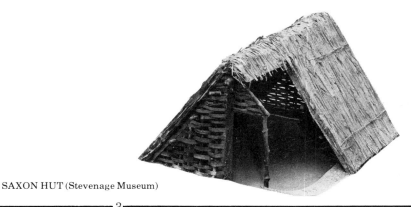

SAXON HUT (Stevenage Museum)

CRUCKS AND BOX FRAMES

Improved skills and tools made it possible to work heavier timbers. Houses became larger and more durable. Some still survive in part from the 13th century. In the lowland areas of England heavy oak timbers were available for building purposes until the beginning of the 17th century, when the supply began to dwindle. The timber-framed buildings which evolved are of two main families.

CRUCKS

Slightly curved main-frame timbers rest on the ground or sill, but meet or are linked to form the apex of the roof. This method of construction was common in the midlands and west of England. Isolated examples are to be found in the western parts of Hertfordshire. Cruck buildings required carefully matched and shaped timbers, and could not easily be extended upwards or sideways. The method was therefore less widely used than the more adaptable box-frame.

WATER END, HEMEL HEMPSTEAD, MOOR COTTAGE
The interior photograph shows a pair of crucks (one beyond the open door) linked at the top by a collar.

BOX FRAME   CRUCK

BOX-FRAMES

Outer walls and the main internal divisions are constructed as rectangular frames and erected on ground-level sills. The length of both cruck-built and box-framed buildings is determined by the number of *bays* or cross-frames. Width is limited by the maximum length of timber available for the transverse tie beams.

FRAMES AND BAYS
(From Discovering Timber-framed Buildings, by Richard Harris. Shire Publications Ltd.)

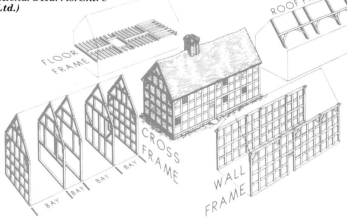

If extra width was needed this would be achieved by providing side aisles. This was most likely to occur in a barn like that at Croxley Green but a few houses also contained aisled halls.

Two ingenious methods, the *hammer-beam* or the *base-cruck*, could be used to support the roof trusses without the need for inconvenient internal posts.

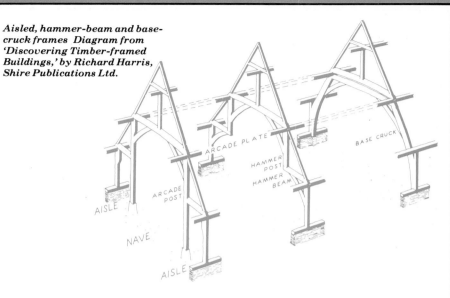

Aisled, hammer-beam and base-cruck frames Diagram from 'Discovering Timber-framed Buildings,' by Richard Harris, Shire Publications Ltd.

WARE. PLACE HOUSE
Aisled hall

FRANK JOEL

OFFLEY. THE OLD POST OFFICE ('COURT HOUSE')
The rear (i.e., right-hand side) wing of this building is a base-cruck hall.

ADRIAN GIBSON

THORLEY. THORLEY HALL.
This is not a true hammer-beam roof. The internal posts in the former aisled hall have been cut away, and the hammer posts are supported by substantial transverse timbers. An upper floor has been inserted.

DEVELOPMENT OF THE 'HALL' HOUSE

T HE EARLIEST timber-framed houses which survive consisted originally of a single-storeyed hall open to the rafters. This undivided area provided accommodation for eating, sleeping and social purposes for the whole household. In the centre was a hearth from which smoke rose into the high roof. Former open halls, however they may have been subsequently adapted, can still be identified by the sooting of the roof timbers.

Private apartments (the *solar*) were an early addition at one end of the communal hall, and service rooms at the other. A *cross passage* passed in front of the service end and provided access to the hall, usually by doors on both sides of the building. Side walls (*screens*) helped to separate the passage from the open hall itself.

The photographs show the pair of doors which, in this part of the country, invariably opened from the cross passage into the two service

A sequence of medieval house styles.
**Diagram from 'Discovering Timber-framed Buildings'
by Richard Harris, Shire Publications Ltd.**

rooms, the *pantry* used for bread, and the *buttery* used for beer. (Note that *buttery* refers to butts, later bottles, not to butter).

In Ware High Street service doors can be traced in the side walls of some of the wagon entries on the west side, showing that these have been driven through former hall houses.

The solar and service areas, being relatively small in size, and unheated, had no need for a high roof as an escape for smoke. A ceiling was

therefore inserted at a convenient height, and the space above used for storage. It was accessible at first by ladder, later by a staircase, from the open hall.

In the 15th and early 16th centuries when these modest changes were taking place, an essential feature of the hall was still the open fire, which burned on a central hearth. It was not yet possible, therefore, to extend the upper floor across the main hall.

THUNDRIDGE. FABDENS

WARE. HIGH STREET

KELSHALL. THE MALTINGS

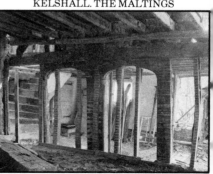

HUNSDON. OLIVE'S FARM.
*A cross passage house in which an upper
floor has later been inserted. Roof
timbers are heavily sooted above the
former open hall.*

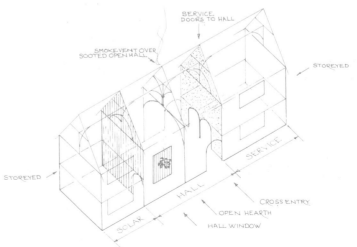

SERVICE
DOORS TO HALL

SMOKE VENT OVER
SOOTED OPEN HALL

STOREYED

STOREYED

SERVICE

HALL

CROSS ENTRY

OPEN HEARTH

SOLAR

HALL WINDOW

ADRIAN GIBSON

CROSS WINGS

The next development was the conversion of the upper floor space above one (or both) of the ends of the hall into a *cross wing*, at right angles to the main axis of the house. This wing was completely partitioned off from the open hall, and was conveniently habitable since it provided additional headroom. It was also *jettied* out to overhang the ground floor on the front, or both front and back, of the building.

MUCH HADHAM.
A small medieval hall house with single cross wing. The later insertion of a floor above the hall itself has been made possible without raising the roof level by the use of two dormer windows

ASHWELL. MILL STREET.
In the building in the foreground, the original hall lies beyond the cross wing. On the near side of the cross wing is a slightly later extension. The height of the roof of the main hall has been raised to accommodate an upper storey.

DANE END.
A double cross wing. The roof of the central hall remains at its original height. One wing has been 'rendered', the other shows recent brick nogging between the timber studs.

KELSHALL. THE MALTINGS.
*Three stages in the restoration of a
derelict cross wing house.*

**The restoration of this building was undertaken by
Hertfordshire Building Preservation Trust.**

THE WEALDEN HOUSE

The complex task of roofing a cross wing house was simplified by providing a continuous roof, wide enough to cover both the jettied cross wings and the recessed centre section with its characteristic coved top. This style of building was most common south of the Thames — hence its name — but several examples are known in Hertfordshire.

THUNDRIDGE. FABDENS.
A Wealden house little altered externally save for the insertion of the chimneys. When the house was first built, probably about 1500, smoke from an open central hearth would have found its way out through the gablets at either end of the roof ridge.
Right, top to bottom: *Wealden houses at Barkway, Walkern and Stevenage.*

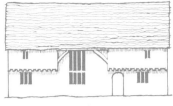
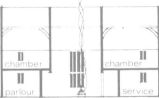
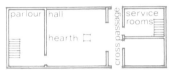

Diagram from 'Timber-framed Buildings' by John Bailey. Beds, Bucks, and Cambs. Historic Building Research Group.

CONTINUOUS JETTIES

A jetty rests on the ends of the joists supporting the upper floor, which are usually exposed. The lower edge of the jetty is supported by a longitudinal timber (*bressumer*). An upper floor does not *require* a jetty, but it seems to have become a fashionable feature in later medieval times.

A continuous jetty can occur only if an upper floor extends across the whole of the central hall. A house with such a jetty must therefore be later in date than the introduction of chimneys, which made this possible (i.e., about the middle of the 16th century).

When an upper floor was inserted into an existing building, it was often necessary to raise the wallplate to increase headroom. Evidence of this can sometimes be seen in the end wall.

FLAUNDEN. OAK COTTAGE.

CODICOTE. BEAM ENDS.

BARKWAY. THE OLD FORGE.

HITCHIN. BRIDGE STREET.
In one bay of this house the bressumer has been cut and raised to allow wagon access to the rear.

OPEN roof vents were never a satisfactory method of extracting smoke. In some open halls an attempt was made to improve the atmosphere by partitioning off a *smoke bay* as a more efficient escape channel. This allowed partial flooring of the upper part of the hall. An improvement on this was a *smoke hood,* which tapered as it rose and came a step closer to being a chimney.

Both smoke bays and smoke hoods were timber-framed and plastered on the inside. Their siting posed difficulties if they were not to impede movement through the house, and they would have constituted a serious fire hazard had they really created an effective draught.

It was a small step forward from wooden smoke hoods to brick-built chimneys. These had been inserted into most old buildings by the end of the 16th century, and were commonly included in new houses thereafter. Convenience and prudence caused many to be built externally, as at the Old Rose and Crown, Braughing.

The commonest location for an inserted chimney stack was between the external doors in the former cross passage, where it required the least structural alteration. The outer door would then open into a small lobby, with the chimney breast ahead and the hall and service area on either side. An alternative position was between the hall and the solar, where the stack could serve both the main

SMOKE BAY · SMOKE HOOD · EXTERNAL CHIMNEY · INTERNAL CHIMNEY

Diagram from 'Discovering Timber-framed Buildings' by Richard Harris, Shire Publications Ltd.

hall and the private apartments.

The insertion of a chimney made it possible to construct an upper floor over the former open hall. The two seem often to have been done simultaneously.

Access to the upper floor was usually by an internal staircase, but sometimes the addition of an external stair turret provided a simpler solution.

The introduction of chimneys made possible a great variety of internal arrangements. Later timber-framed houses did not necessarily conform to any of the standard medieval patterns.

HARE STREET. BELL COTTAGES.

BRAUGHING. THE OLD ROSE AND CROWN.
The smoke bay is in a rear wing of this building. The external chimney in the front range is contemporary with that part of the building, which also has a continuous jetty.

GREAT HORMEAD
Towering and finely decorated chimneys were adopted, like jetties, as fashionable embellishments in the 16th century.

BARKWAY. 2 HIGH STREET
A timber-framed smoke hood occupies one end of the hall, with a through passage on the left. An inserted floor is supported above the lintel. The smoke hood seems to have been added soon after the house was built in the 16th century since there is only light sooting of the rafters. The upper floor was inserted somewhat later, probably after 1600.

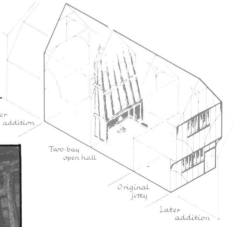

Later addition
Two-bay open hall
Original jetty
Later addition

BUILDING IN TIMBER: CONSTRUCTION & EMBELLISHMENT

PATTERNS OF FRAMES & BRACES

LOWER PEOVER, CHESHIRE
Rectangular frame pattern with 'arch' braces, characteristic of the midlands and north west of England, but sometimes found in Hertfordshire.

BRAUGHING
'Tension' braces rising from a horizontal beam, the more common arrangement in the south east.

VINE COTTAGE, MUCH HADHAM
Vertical close studding, fashionable in East Anglia in the 16th and 17th centuries. (centre part of building). Braces, visible in the left-hand building, were then hidden behind the plaster to avoid spoiling the decorative effect.

GREEN TYE, MUCH HADHAM
The use of less substantial timbers indicates that this building was extended to the right in the late 17th century, when timber supplies were dwindling.

TREATMENT OF TIMBERS

GRAVELEY
Until about 1700 wood was left in its natural state.

HARE STREET
In the late 18th century timbers were often hidden by 'rendering', partly to improve weatherproofing but also because this became a fashionable style.

HARE STREET
From about 1860 timbers were again exposed, and coloured black to contrast with white-painted plaster. Many early buildings were 'restored' during this period.

HARPENDEN
Timber-framing has continued to be employed in the construction of many newly-built houses, usually in gables or upper storeys only. Sometimes non-structural timber patterns are applied as decoration ('Mock-Tudor').

THATCH

*The natural roof covering, used from earliest times. Materials vary
from region to region: water reed is used in much of East Anglia, but
long-stemmed wheat straw is most common in Hertfordshire*

RENT PELHAM	STOCKING PELHAM	ANSTEY	FURNEUX PELHAM

*Four photographs showing the style which predominates in
Essex and the north-east of Hertfordshire. The thatch is wrapped
round the half-hipped ends of the roof, and distinctive up-turned tips
at the ends of the ridge are a reminder of former smoke vents.*

REED	BARKWAY	COTTERED	FURNEUX PELHAM

*Four photographs showing some of the ridge patterns which
can help to identify individual craftsmen.*

AFTER the Roman period, brickmaking in this country did not revive until the 15th century. It was not easy to transport bricks far from their kilns, and they were usually made from locally available clay. Sizes varied: the first standard dimensions (9 x $4\frac{1}{2}$ x $2\frac{1}{4}$ inches) were laid down by statute in 1571.

Hertfordshire's earliest prestige buildings in the new materials included:

HODDESDON. RYE HOUSE. (c. 1443).

HERTFORD. THE CASTLE GATEHOUSE. (c. 1460)

HATFIELD. THE OLD PALACE (1480-90)

COURTESY OF THE MARQUESS OF SALISBURY

The more common use of brick was stimulated after 1550 by the need to construct fireproof chimneys in timber-framed buildings.

The period from 1550 to 1620 has been called 'The Great Rebuilding'. Large numbers of timber-framed houses were rebuilt at that time, either in the grander new timber styles or in brick.

At first the use of brick was confined to the wealthy and fashionable classes, but during the next two centuries it moved steadily down the social scale.

COTTERED LORDSHIP
Exterior chimney.

THUNDRIDGE. FABDENS.
Interior chimney, inserted close to the main tie beam and crown post.

BRICK HOUSES OF THE 16th CENTURY

Standon Lordship. (1546)

Little Gaddesdon Manor House (1576)

BRICK HOUSES OF THE 17th CENTURY

Hertford. Balls Park. (c. 1640)

Harpenden, Mackerye End (1665)

BRICK HOUSES OF THE EARLY 18th CENTURY

Sawbridgeworth. The Red House.

Hertford. Bayley Hall.

BONDING BRICKWORK

Various methods of bonding could be used in different circumstances, or merely for effect:

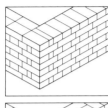

ENGLISH BOND

FLEMISH BOND

GARDEN WALL BOND

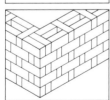

RAT-TRAP BOND

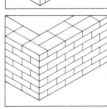

STRETCHER BOND

From Hertfordshire Conservation File: Bricks in Hertfordshire. (HCC, 1983)

In 1828 Caleb Hitch of Ware patented a method of building using bricks of various shapes and sizes, with interlocking flanges designed to save mortar and increase strength. They were used in building many houses in Ware and its vicinity.

WARE. WATTON ROAD.

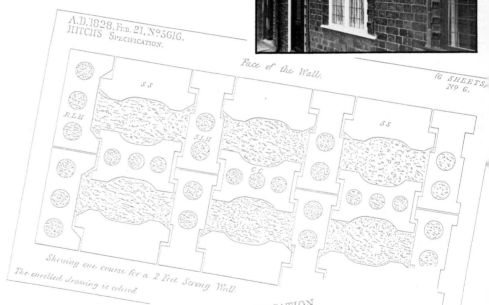

A.D. 1828, Feb. 21, N° 5616.
HITCH'S SPECIFICATION.

Face of the Wall.

(6 SHEETS)
N° 6.

Showing one course for a 2 Feet Strong Wall.
The enrolled drawing is colored.

HITCH'S SPECIFICATION.

TO ALL TO WHOM TEESE PRESENTS SHALL COME, I, CALEB HITCH the younger, of Ware, in the County of Hertford, Brickmaker, send greeting.

5   WHEREAS His present most Excellent Majesty King George the Fourth, by His Letters Patent under the Great Seal of Great Britain, bearing date at Westminster, the Twenty-first day of February, in the ninth year of His reign, did, for Himself, His heirs and successors, give and grant unto me, the said Caleb Hitch the younger, His especial licence that I, the said Caleb Hitch the younger, my ex̄ors, adm̄ors, and assigns, or such others as I, the said

10 Caleb Hitch the younger, my ex̄ors, adm̄ors, or assigns, should at any time agree with, and no others, from time to time and at all times thereafter during

—— 1767 ——
Improvement of the Lea Navigation made it easier to bring bulky cargoes up to Hertford.

—— 1797 ——
The Grand Junction Canal from Brentford reached Hemel Hempstead. it reached Tring in 1799, and the industrial midlands a few years later.

—— 1837 ——
The London & Birmingham Railway reached Tring. The Great Eastern Railway served Bishop's Stortford by 1842 and Hertford East by 1843. The Great Northern Railway through Hatfield and Hitchin opened in 1850.

THE AVAILABILITY of building materials was transformed by these developments. House builders were no longer limited to using the materials immediately to hand. Bricks could be fired with coal instead of charcoal, and need no longer be red in colour.

1 ST ANDREW'S STREET.
Single-storeyed cottage, its 16th century timbers concealed by rendering.

2 WEST STREET
17th century timber-framed house clad with weatherboard.

3 NICHOLAS LANE.
Timber-framed house with a red-brick facade added before 1767.

4 WEST STREET.
A post-1767 house of yellow stock bricks, with slate roof and concealed window frames.

5 St. ANDREW'S STREET.
17th century house with yellow brick facade and concealed sash frames of the late 18th century.

6 ST. ANDREW'S STREET
Tiled roof and 18th century sash windows in exposed frames, inserted into a 16th century cross-wing house (centre right).

HOUSES IN HERTFORD: THE TRANSITION FROM TIMBER TO BRICK

Before 1767, when the Lea Navigation was improved, houses in the town were predominantly timber-framed with steeply pitched red-tiled roofs.

After the improvement of the Lea Navigation in 1767, new buildings in Hertford were almost entirely of brick, with low-pitched slate roofs.

Other timber-framed buildings in Hertford which were given brick facades and other fashionable *improvements* during this period of transition.

THE PROVISION OF FRESH WATER

THE need for access to water from surface streams or ponds, or from wells, mainly determined early settlement sites. Pumps were introduced from about 1500, to serve whole villages or individual houses. As needs increased, new methods were adopted. Fresh water was brought to Hoddesdon by conduit in 1620; from 1631 London received a supply of Hertfordshire water by means of the *New River.* The Victorians' eventual recognition of the link between health and sanitation led to a great increase in provision of uncontaminated water supplies during the 19th century.

The provision of piped water, available from taps in individual houses, became common in towns by the end of the 19th century, and is now almost universal even in rural areas.

The ability to obtain fresh water by turning a tap is an important element in civilised living

So is the convenience of the modern W.C.

HUNSDON.

ARDELEY.
This village green, with thatched houses and a covered well, was designed and built in 1917.

HADHAM FORD
Pump 'Erected by subscription April 1860'

THE DISPOSAL OF WASTE

Chamber pots have been widely used since medieval times, though some important medieval houses contained a fixed privy which drained directly into a sewage pit. The mid-18th century saw the common use of commodes in elegant houses, and elsewhere the provision of outside privies. These were usually situated at the bottom of the garden. They consisted of a shed containing a hinged seat over a hole in the ground or a bucket which had to be emptied by hand. They have remained in fairly wide use within living memory.

The earth closet, invented by the Revd Henry Moule in 1860, eliminated the most unsavoury features of the simple privy. A hinged seat lay over a bucket in similar fashion, but behind it was a hopper filled with dry earth, charcoal or ashes. Raising the handle at the front allowed a layer of this material to fall into the bucket rendering its

In 1877, S.S. Hellyer wrote, in *The Plumber and Sanitary Houses:*

"In every house a water-closet may be considered a necessity, and a slop sink a convenience. By English people lavatories [i.e., wash-basins] and baths fitted up with hot and cold services would I suppose be considered a luxury ...".

Hellyer gave the following advice on installing water-closets in existing houses:

"No water-closet should be fitted up in a room which cannot be well lighted and ventilated, i.e., all water-closet rooms should be built outside the main walls of the house or should have an external wall for one of its sides, so that a large window may be put in for light and air ...".

WESTON. THE OLD FORGE.
Earth closet (now in Hitchin Museum).

contents sterile in a short time.

Flushing water closets, first patented in 1775, were widely used in fashionable houses by 1814, draining to a cess pit. They did not come into common use, however, until near the end of the 19th century.

THERFIELD. DANE END
Back garden privies (disused).

BRICK HOUSES AND HOUSE PLANS

DESIGNS for a block of four tenements, prepared with the encouragement of Prince Albert, were exhibited at the great Exhibition of 1851. They were intended "to promote the much needed improvement of the dwellings of the working classes". Several such blocks were built, including these two in Hertfordshire.

HERTFORD, COWBRIDGE.

In its very early days, in 1905, Letchworth Garden City sponsored a *Cheap Cottages Exhibition* — none to cost more than £150. Many of the exhibits are still in good shape, in Icknield Way and Nevells Road (then called Exhibition Road).

ABBOTTS LANGLEY.

LETCHWORTH

Plans and photographs on the following pages show some representative houses of the early 20th century.

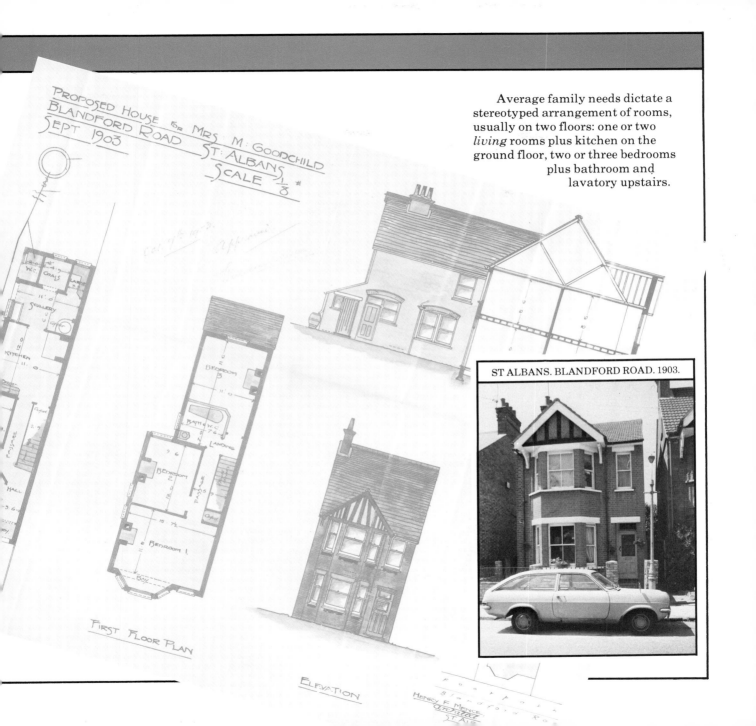

Average family needs dictate a stereotyped arrangement of rooms, usually on two floors: one or two *living* rooms plus kitchen on the ground floor, two or three bedrooms plus bathroom and lavatory upstairs.

PROPOSED HOUSE FOR MRS M: GOODCHILD
BLANDFORD ROAD St: ALBANS
SEPT 1903
SCALE ⅛"

W.C. COALS
SCULLERY
KITCHEN
PASSAGE
HALL

BEDROOM 3
BATH & W.C.
LANDING
BEDROOM 2
BEDROOM 1
BAY

FIRST FLOOR PLAN

ELEVATION

ST ALBANS. BLANDFORD ROAD. 1903.

HENRY F. MENCE ARCHITECT
ST ALB

The growth of towns has been possible partly through the provision of relatively cheap terrace housing, economical in space but providing usually only limited amenities.

ST ALBANS. CAMBRIDGE ROAD 1912.

The apartments and tenements of the 19th century gave way in the 20th century to flats and maisonettes, sometimes situated above shops.

Road Elevation

Section AB.

HITCHIN. HERMITAGE ROAD. 1926.

ancroft Elevation

Single-storeyed bungalows found
some favour in the 1930s.

4 SEMI-DETACHED·BUNGALOWS AT LONGACRES, ST.ALBANS.
FOR P. BUTTERFIELD (ST ALBANS) LTD.

6291

Scale ~ 8 FEET TO INCH

FRONT ELEVATION

BACK ELEVATION

LETCHWORTH.

In the mid-
1940s a high standard of design
enabled them to achieve
unexpected popular success as
post-war *prefabs*.

SITTING
ROOM

BEDROOM

KITCHEN

SITTING
ROOM

ST ALBANS. LONGACRES. 1938.

PLAN

47·0
23·6
24×3
12×9

Before the 1914-18 war, town houses of three storeys accommodated living-in servants. Now they are more likely to result from the desire to provide as many dwellings as possible — often including garages — on restricted sites.

The cost of heating is a major factor in determining the size of rooms and windows. After a long flirtation with glass walls and open planning, cozier rooms with small windows to improve insulation are now again in favour.

HERTFORD. ST. ANDREW'S STREET. 18th CENTURY.

ST ALBANS. BEACONSFIELD ROAD. 1903.

CHIPPERFIELD. LITTLE WINCH. 1935.

DEREK PHILIPS

HARPENDEN. STATION ROAD. 1979.

HATFIELD. OLD RECTORY DRIVE. 1975.

THE EMBELLISHMENT OF BRICK BUILDINGS

THE MAIN beauty of a brick facade lies in the proportions and patterns of windows and doors, and the quality of the brickwork itself.

Bricks fired by charcoal (mostly before 1770) were normally red in colour. A blue finish could be produced by vitrifaction to provide a striking contrast. Urquhart House opposite, was enriched in this way. Many of the finer farmhouses and town houses were similarly treated.

Since the late 18th century the firing of bricks at higher temperatures through the use of coal has increased the scope for producing patterns of different coloured bricks.

BUNTINGFORD. URQUHART HOUSE

Hadham Ford. On the right, quoins, window surrounds and selected courses have been picked out in yellow to add interest to a red brick building. The house on the left has the date (1866) and other patterns in blue.

BATFORD
LOWER LUTON ROAD

HATFIELD.
FORE STREET

BALDOCK

POPULATION GROWTH

1851	167,000
1951	610,000
1982	955,000

THIS RATE of growth has called for more new houses than could be provided in ones and twos in the traditional way. Private and local authority *housing estates* have met some of the demand. Hertfordshire has also been the location of two new Garden Cities and three New Towns. Public transport and the growth of car ownership have reduced the need for people to live within a mile or two of their work: proximity to a bus stop or a railway station is often more relevant. The need to garage the family car now influences the planning of new houses and causes additions to be made to many old ones.

AEROFILMS LTD

BERKHAMSTED.
Looking north. Across the centre run the A41 road, the Grand Union Canal, and the railway.

In the foreground is mainly 19th century development, including some terraces of three or four houses, and some in-filling during the 1920s and 1930s. The whole of this area was built before the boom in car ownership: garages were not normally provided, but several can be seen to have been added. Where there is no room for this, cars are left in the street.

Beyond the railway a large post-war housing development provides a choice of two basic designs. Each house has its own garage, approached by a drive from the road.

Hertfordshire has very few tower blocks of flats. This one is in Stevenage. The method of construction, using a steel or reinforced concrete frame instead of load-bearing walls, brings us full circle, back to the principles which governed timber-framed building in medieval times.

G.L. BLAKE

SELECTED BOOKS FOR FURTHER READING

TIMBER-FRAMED BUILDINGS
JOHN BAILEY
Bedfordshire, Buckinghamshire and
Cambridgeshire Historic Building
Research Group, 1979
£1.50

ILLUSTRATED HANDBOOK OF VERNACULAR ARCHITECTURE
R. W. BRUNSKILL
2nd Edition, Faber 1978
Paperback £2.95

DISCOVERING TIMBER-FRAMED BUILDINGS
RICHARD HARRIS
Shire Publications 1978
85p

HERTFORDSHIRE (THE BUILDINGS OF ENGLAND SERIES)
NIKOLAUS PEVSNER
2nd Edition. Revised by Bridget Cherry
Penguin Books, 1977
£4.75

YOUR HOUSE THE OUTSIDE VIEW
JOHN PRIZEMAN
2nd Edition. Quiller Press,1982
£5.95

ACKNOWLEDGEMENTS

This handbook complements an exhibition sponsored by the Standing Committee for Museum Services in Hertfordshire. We wish to acknowledge practical assistance received from the curators of the District Council Museums, and from the Planning Department of Hertfordshire County Council; advice and guidance generously given by Adrian Gibson and by very many others; and the loan of photographs from many sources. Wherever possible, credit has been given to original photographers. We apologise to any who have inadvertently been omitted. Most unacknowledged photographs, however, are from County Council collections,or provided by the author.

The cost of photography for the exhibition, and for this publication, has been borne partly by donations from the following

Redland Aggregates Ltd.,
Woolmer Green, Knebworth, Herts. SG3 6LF

Marconi Avionics Ltd.,
Elstree Way, Borehamwood, Herts.WD6 1RX

Grays (Hatfield) Ltd.,
1, Great North Road,Hatfield,Herts. AL9 5JA

Merck Sharp & Dohme Ltd.,
Hertford Road, Hoddesdon, Herts. EN11 9BU

Stortford Fitted Interiors Ltd.,
37, Hockerill Street, Bishop's Stortford, Herts

McMullen & Sons Ltd.,
The Hertford Brewery, Hertford,
Herts SG14 1RD.

Smith Kline & French Laboratories Ltd.
Welwyn Garden City, Herts. AL7 1EY.

Designed by:
David Kolakowski

Typset in Century Schoolbook by:
Cleer Typesetters, Hertford

Printed by:
The Burlington Press (Cambridge) Ltd

HERTFORDSHIRE PUBLICATIONS

(HERTFORDSHIRE LIBRARY SERVICE AND HERTFORDSHIRE LOCAL HISTORY COUNCIL
EAST DIVISION LIBRARY HEADQUARTERS
38 HIGH STREET,
STEVENAGE OLD TOWN,
HERTFORDSHIRE

© 1984 ARTHUR JONES
ISBN 0 901354 295